FORCED™ ABSENCE

The Screenplay

FORCED™ ABSENCE

A Story About Children of Divorce, Child Support, Custody, and Parental Alienation Wars.

By

PIUS A. UZAMERE

Published by Vilu-Plag
Sharon

Copyright © 2014 by Vilu-Plag.
All rights reserved under International and Pan-American Copyright Conventions. This screenplay is a derivative of the feature motion picture: FORCED ABSENCE. Copyright © 2014, Equilibrium Entertainment Corp. All rights reserved.

The lyrics referenced in this screenplay are from "FORCED ABSENCE - The original theatrical soundtrack" performed by The Mighty Hellbenderz Band on EEC Records & Interactives label. Published by Des Maraf Music Publishing Co, ASCAP. Copyright© 2008- 2014, Equilibrium Entertainment Corp. All rights reserved. Grateful acknowledgment is made to all the entities named above.

ISBN-10 : 1892662035
ISBN-13 : 978-1-892662-03-3

Library of Congress Control Number: 2014918820

DEDICATION

This work is dedicated to all children who are denied their fundamental rights to the love, nurture, comfort, and care of their non-custodial parents but don't know why.

It is also dedicated to the non-abusive mothers and fathers whose unending fight for equal access to their children will hopefully lead to the eradication of judicially imposed mental, emotional and psychological abuse of children.

PREFACE

The Journey to Forced Absence

While in the midst of pre-production for another film, I saw a horrific news clip. A man shot his ex-wife and then turned the gun on himself, orphaning their two children. It appears that their dad was frustrated with unaffordable child support and minimal visitation rights. Reporters alluded to the fact that he'd had a rough childhood and no father figure in his life.

I was struck by the plight of those orphans. How would they cope? Who could ever reverse the psychological trauma, fill the void in their little hearts, shield their fragile minds from the turbulent nightmares that await them and be persuasive enough to make them believe that happier days and years await them? Although I shuddered at the implication that a bad childhood should excuse a sociopath from being responsible for committing a murder, I wondered how exactly their father morphed from who he was during the lovey dovey days of their courtship, and what he ended up being: her murderer who plunged his own children into a hellish abyss.

This incident, and others like it, drove me to research post nuptial conflicts and their effects on children, their parents, and society. To help me understand the depth of the problems, I organized a national conference on dual parenting, and commissioned research papers by psychiatrists, psychologists, sociologists, lawyers and social workers. I attended hundreds hearings in multiple jurisdictions over several years.

As the research progressed, I realized that those of us who have been spared the bitter taste of contentious and acrimonious divorces are mostly oblivious to the horrors lurking in the underbelly of this beast. The process subjects children and their parents to a startling amount of stress, venom, mental anguish, and financial hardship due to oppressive laws enforced by a corrupt and or ineffectual family court system.

I decided to tell the story of the thousands of families impacted by the family court system. I distilled the material gathered over more than a dozen years into a better-than-fiction feature documentary. *Forced Absence* is my attempt to shed some light on the family court systems.

Pius A Uzamere

Acknowledgment

Special Thanks To:

Jeff Bowen, LISW, M. Ed (Psych)
Rhonda Hartman J.D.
Maurice Heidish, MSW
Dr. Robert Howland, M.D.
Dr. Fred Radfer, M.D.
Albert Whale
Robert Mendelson
Mark and Deborah Collins
The Tangiers Bar
Fat E's
Greg and Tammie Wormley
Jean Osborne
Randy Bass and Lisa Grafton
Michael D. Simon
Debbie Varney - Simon

"FORCED ABSENCE"

FADE IN:
EXT. BUSY STREET - EVENING

We open with cars driving down a busy four lane street. We see, and follow, a minivan for a couple of blocks. It makes a right turn into the parking lot of a restaurant/pub. Ed Williams steps out of the car carrying a portfolio. His cell phone rings. Ed puts his portfolio back in the car and answers the phone, leaning against his car.

CUT TO:
INT. CLUB/RESTAURANT LOBBY - EVENING

The lobby is a well-appointed space with a sitting area overlooking the bar and dining area. On the walls are several pieces of custom artwork. At the far end of the lobby are club chairs and sofas for guests waiting to be seated. Closer to the entrance is a hostess' station. The hostess is at her station arranging her menu. ANDREA, a lady in her late

Forced Absence / 2

twenties, enters and approaches the HOSTESS. MRS. ANDREA NEWTON, a twenty-something woman, enters. She quickly scans the lounge area and glances at the band playing WORDS UNSPOKEN. The HOSTESS approaches her.

              WORDS UNSPOKEN
I see the tears in my eyes, but why can't I see
The woman, the friend, the lover I used to be
I've always been beside you, was the best I could be
You can't look me in the eye and tell me that you still want me (more)

                  HOSTESS
        Welcome to the Attic.
            (beat)
        Is it just one today?

                  ANDREA
        My name is Andrea Newton. I'm
        supposed to meet Ed Williams
        here. Do you know him?

                  HOSTESS
        Yes, he's one of our regulars. He
        called about 15 minutes ago
        saying he'll be 10 minutes late. Do
        you want to sit at the bar or at a
        table?

                    ANDREA
          The bar is good.

                    HOSTESS
          May I get you anything?

                    ANDREA
          Maybe later.

They walk toward the bar with the hostess leading the way.

INT. THE ATTIC BAR - EVENING

The bar is thirty feet wide and semicircular with leather padded seats around. It is rustic, but elegant, with a mixed clientele of factory and mid-level management office workers. The bartender is busy mixing drinks while a dozen or so patrons enjoy their drinks and watch the performance to the left of the bar.

The HOSTESS pulls a chair for ANDREA.

                    ANDREA
          Thanks. These guys are good.

                    HOSTESS
                    (smiling)
          Oh, yes. THE MIGHTY
          HELLBENDERZ BAND is very
          good. They're just warming up. By

Forced Absence / 4

      tonight, this place will be packed.

CUT TO:
INT. THE STAGE - DAY

THE MIGHTY HELLBENDERZ BAND, featuring Debbie Varney Simon, is on stage playing "WORDS UNSPOKEN." Debbie is at the microphone.

      WORDS UNSPOKEN
I keep playing it over and over again in my head
Was it something I didn't do, or just something I never said?
I don't want to be alone, but baby are we too far gone?
You can't break the silence with words unspoken
Do we just go on believing this heart can stay unbroken?

I know that you love me. I don't like feeling demanded
And, you should know that you can't take a woman's love for granted
I've been too long alone. Too many nights left crying
If you love me so long, why can't you see a part of me is dying?

CUT TO:
EXT. TIM'S HOUSE - EVENING

We start with a medium close on the entrance and

porch, and then zoom out to reveal the tranquility: acres of green grass dotted with fruit trees. We pan slowly left and find a car parked by the side entrance.

EXT. CAR INTERIOR - EVENING

TIM is sitting on the driver's seat surrounded by a bunch of plastic sandwich bags. In them are several tablets and capsules of varying sizes and colors. He is holding a half-full whiskey bottle which he uses to chase down the pills. On the front passenger seat is a revolver.

CUT TO:
INT. CLUB/RESTAURANT LOBBY - EVENING

The hostess returns to her mark and sees ED WILLIAMS coming in as the band is finishing WORDS UNSPOKEN.

>   HOSTESS
> Hi, ED. She's here at the bar
> waiting for you.

>   ED WILLIAMS
> Thanks.

ED goes to GREG, RANDY, and DEBBI and shakes their hands.

> ED WILLIAMS
> THE MIGHTY HELLBENDERZ
> BAND is destined for greatness.
> Mark my words.

> GREGORY
> Thanks, Ed.

> RANDY
> You're a little early today, aren't you?

> ED WILLIAMS
> Still on the job. Still on the job.

DEBBIE exits the stage as RANDY takes the mic closer to him. THE MIGHTY HELLBENDERZ starts playing SEPARATE WAYS - THE THEME FROM FORCED ABSENCE.

> SEPARATE WAYS - THE THEME FROM *FORCED ABSENCE*

At the end of the night
Would you turn out the light?
Would you leave me out in the cold?
At the end of the day
No more words to say
I want to see my kids before I get old

For every five things that I've done wrong
I can name five for you in this song

Why don't we just make amends?
For every ten things that I didn't do
I could name eleven more you didn't do too
Just go our separate ways just as friends

The hostess takes ED to ANDREA.

>   HOSTESS
> ED, this is ANDREA NEWTON.

ED shakes her hand.

>   ED WILLIAMS
> Hi, I'm ED WILLIAMS, and it's a
> real pleasure, MRS. NEWTON.

>   ANDREA
> Nice to meet you. My attorney
> spoke highly of you.

>   ED WILLIAMS
> LEENA is a great client and a
> friend.
>   (Pointing at the booth)
> MRS. NEWTON, why don't we sit
> over there so we can talk freely
> and privately?

The two move to a more secluded area.

ANDREA
Andrea, please.

ED WILLIAMS
I'll call you Andrea, and you can call me ED. ANDREA, LEENA hired me to further investigate issues relating to your case. When the court awarded sole custody of your children to your ex, the judge used a set of metrics to determine what is in the best interest of the children. My job is to develop a new set of metrics that will compel the judge to reverse himself and opt for co-parenting with equal access and input into the rearing of these kids. There is absolutely no assurance that I will succeed. I hope that you understand that?

ANDREA
I do.

ED WILLIAMS
One thing I can promise is that I will do my darndest to help in any way possible.

                    ANDREA
            I like that. Well, just tell me what I
            need to do, and I'll do it.

CUT TO:
EXT. CARMICHAEL'S RESIDENCE - DAY

A television crew is on site broadcasting.

                    NEWS REPORTER
            In August 1996, the tranquility of
            this quiet community was
            shattered by several gunshot
            blasts. Within minutes, county and
            city police converged on the
            house at 3234 Livermore. What
            they found was one of the
            bloodiest crime scenes in this
            city's history. Dead were John P.
            Carmichael (25), his wife Jane X
            Carmichael (39), and her two
            daughters from her second
            marriage. After extensive
            investigations lasting more than a
            year, police arrested TIM OLSON
            (20), Mrs. Carmichael's son from
            her first marriage. Although the
            defendant refused to testify or
            cooperate with his court-
            appointed attorney, this sad
            chapter came to an end with:

Forced Absence / 10

CUT TO:
INT. COUNTY COURTROOM #1 - DAY

The JUDGE is sitting behind the bench with a gavel in hand addressing TIM, who is in a prison garb, standing with handcuffs, chains, and leg irons.

> JUDGE
> It is my sentence that you'll be put to death by lethal injection. This court is in recess.

We see a close up of the gavel as it strikes the plate.

> BAILIFF
> All, rise.

The judge leaves for his chamber.
LEENA, the court appointed attorney, and the prosecutor walk quietly out of the courtroom, neither acknowledging the other.

CUT TO:
INT. POST OFFICE LOBBY - DAY

LEENA is at the post office clearing her box. She sorts through the mail, discards the junk mail, and puts the rest in her brief case with the exception of a #10 envelope which she opens and reads. We hear the voice of TIM (the inmate) reading a letter that he sent to LEENA as she walks to the jail.

> TIM (o.s)
> Dear LEENA,
>
> Just a note to let you know that I truly appreciate your tireless effort in trying to do the impossible: free me from the death sentence. However1111 altruistic the notion of snatching a man from the jaws of death is, it is neither welcomed, desired, nor accepted. I'm quite at peace with my sentence; partly because I deserve it, but mostly because I'm fucking tired of living. I have lived, and I hate it. Now, I'm anxious to try death and the afterlife. For all practical purposes, my life ended several years ago, well before I killed my mother, sisters, and stepfather. So, please stop all the legal research, brief writing, and countless motions. For the past several months, the only joy in my life has been you. I have never met anyone quite like you. Your inner grace and beauty coupled with your warmth, grace, and caring heart have enriched my life immensely. Every week you come

Forced Absence / 12

here, you ask if there is something you can get for me? Cigarettes, magazines, etc. My answer has always been the same: no! Here is the truth. Don't send me cigarettes unless they are fortified with your personal scent so I can smell you day and night. Don't send me magazines unless every page is filled with your photographs so I can see more of you day and night. Finally, if I could have one wish granted, it wouldn't be for freedom 'cause freedom is too vain. Rather, it would be for a chance to spend one night with you. Why, you might ask? Intimacy with you will be so gratifying as to crystallize on my face a smile so hearty as to fool the gatekeepers of the afterlife to let me into heaven instead of hell.

Very truly yours,

TIM

CUT TO:
INT. JAIL - DAY

LEENA enters the jail complex and goes to the desk. She signs her name.

> GUARD
> May I help you?

> LEENA
> I'm here to see my client, TIM OLSON.

> GUARD
> You can go into the conference room. I'll go get him.

CUT TO:
INT. ATTORNEY'S MEETING ROOM - DAY

We follow LEENA as she goes to the waiting room. She paces the room while waiting. We hear the remaining portion of TIM's letter.

The guard brings TIM into the attorney's interview room and takes off his handcuffs.

> GUARD
> MS. THOMPSON, I'll be outside.

> LEENA
> Thank you.

The deputy leaves the room and shuts the door.

Forced Absence / 14

LEENA locks it.

> TIM
> Hi.

LEENA stares straight at him and slaps him.

> LEENA
> How dare you toy with my emotions with all your bullshit!

> TIM
> I'm not toying with you.

LEENA takes out the letter, and throws it at him.

> LEENA
> What do you call this?

> TIM
> That's how I feel, alright?

> LEENA
> For the past several months that I've been on your case, you've refused to actively participate in your appeal process. You want me to care about you, but then you want to be executed.

> TIM
> I didn't say that....

Before he could finish his sentence, LEENA pulls him closer and starts caressing his face. She slowly strokes his forehead continuously with the back of her fingers while whispering:

> LEENA
> I'm not giving up on you. I'm going to get you out of here. I'll fight with all of my skills.

Each successive stroke reddens his face more and more. She proceeds to kiss him. First, on one of his waterlogged eyes, then on the lips. TIM couldn't believe LEENA's passionate response to his missive. He momentarily recoils from her clutch for a reality check triggered partly by his apprehension about the worth and potency of his written words but more by the overwhelming nature of his own insecurity. A split second later, he is back in her arms, knowing that an opportunity for a romantic interlude, culminating in sexual contact with an attorney inside a jail, is a rarity that could possibly never avail itself again. She starts to unbutton his shirt while he helps her out of her blouse and bra. They proceed to have sex.

Forced Absence / 16

DISSOLVE TO:
EXT. LEENA'S CAR ON A BUSY STREET - DAY

LEENA in her car. We follow as she drives to a restaurant while "I'LL BE FINE" by THE MIGHTY HELLBENDERZ BAND plays.

I'LL BE FINE

*There's a time and a place for having a fight
And this one here is not all right
'Cause I don't want to see them kids get hurt
When you're back stabbing me and digging up dirt*

*The sooner we sort this out, I'll be just fine
The sooner we sort this out, I'll be just fine*

*Word around town is that you have been putting me down
Just remember what comes around
Goes around, and I'll get mine
And you'll get yours, when you see the sign*

*The sooner we sort this out, I'll be just fine
The sooner we sort this out, I'll be just fine*

*You keep the kids from me and that's just wrong
What we created didn't take very long
Now, you go your way, and I'll go mine
Just give me some time, don't feed me that line*

*The sooner we work this out, I'll be just fine
The sooner we work this out, I'll be just fine*

Well, I gave you keys to the trailer and truck
I didn't even get a kiss for good luck
Makes me smile when you walk away
Sun comes up on a brand new day

The sooner we work this out, I'll be just fine. (x4)

CUT TO:
INT. VILLANOVA RESTAURANT - DAY

LEENA and ROSE are in a booth chit chatting while waiting to be served.

>ROSE
>
>So, how old is your newly found lover?

>LEENA
>
>Twenty.

>ROSE
>
>Did you have him checked out? This mystery lover could be a gigolo or a mass murderer.

LEENA stares at her with a corroborative flair.

>ROSE
>(shaking her head)
>Oh my God. No! No! It's not him.

LEENA
(Nodding and smiling)
Yep. It's him.

ROSE
You've got to stop now, while you still can.

LEENA
I don't want to stop.

ROSE
You'll put your entire career and life in jeopardy. What will Roy say when he finds out?

LEENA
I don't care.

ROSE
You don't care about your marriage?

LEENA
I asked Roy for a no fault divorce.

ROSE
Oh my God, you're losing It. LEENA, I know a good shrink who makes house calls for absolute confidentiality.

>   LEENA
> ROSE, I'm fine. I'm not crazy. I'm
> in love.
>
>   ROSE
> With a murderer?
>
>   LEENA
> He's innocent.
>
>   ROSE
> He confessed, for Christ's sake.
>
>   LEENA
> The confession is invalid.
>
>   ROSE
> The jury convicted him.
>
>   LEENA
> It will be overturned.
>
>   ROSE
> What is the attraction?
>
>   LEENA
> He's funny, passionate, and
> gentle.

ROSE
Gentle enough to kill his own mother.

LEENA
He was suffering from diminished mental capacity. You need to understand the real man behind the headlines.

ROSE
What do you hope to accomplish with this romance? I know what's in it for him – sex. After all, in this state, convicted murderers don't get time off for good behavior. But, what's in it for you?

LEENA
This romance is not about that. Knowing that he loves me, wants me, and needs me is enough for me.

ROSE
What about your husband and children? They love, want, and need you, don't they?

LEENA
In their own ways maybe they do. Well, I guess they do. But, this is

different. With TIM, my life has a purpose and a meaning. Every extra day that I keep him alive is a major accomplishment. Every brief, every motion, every oral argument is full of passion and tremendous energy that propels me into the stratosphere with emotional high. It's like having a continuous orgasm throughout your work day.

ROSE smiles and shakes her head.

ROSE
Wow. I don't know what to say.

LEENA
You don't need to say anything.

ROSE
Don't you feel the same passion for your family?

LEENA
The value, the effect, and the relevancy are not on the same level. "What's his face" is so successful that even when I win a big case, it's nothing but a tiny bleep on the family radar screen.

And even so, my accomplishments in court have no effect, value, or relevancy on "what's his face" and the kids. I love helping people. I want to make a difference in the lives of the oppressed, disenfranchised, and the wrongfully convicted. This is what I'm passionate about.

                    ROSE
"What's his face?" Lena, he has a name. It is Roy THOMPSON - your husband of ten years.

                    LEENA
Soon to be an ex-husband.

                    ROSE
How do you plan to live together? How fulfilling a romance will it be with him in jail?

                    LEENA
I know that I can get him off.

                    ROSE
How?

                    LEENA
By all accounts, TIM was normal

until his parents divorced. In the turf war that followed, TIM sustained emotional scars which fueled his anger. For the next several weeks, I plan on interviewing mental health experts and organizations with experience in this area.

ROSE
The only organization I can think of is the Dual Parenthood Institute. They provide support for non-custodial parents. You may want to attend one of their conferences. Conference attendees usually include educators, professionals in various fields of interests to non-custodial parents.

LEENA
Thanks, this is very helpful. Do you have a phone number or address?

ROSE
They have a website. Dual Parenthood dot something.
(beat)
Well, we better order. I'm starved.

Forced Absence / 24

                    LEENA
            Thanks. Waitress!

A waitress approaches the table.

CUT TO:
INT. LAW OFFICE - DAY

LEENA is sitting at her desk making a phone call.

CUT TO:
INT. OFFICE OF WILLIAMS INVESTIGATIONS

MR. ED WILLIAMS is seated at his desk working. The phone rings. He answers it.

                ED WILLIAMS
        Williams Investigations, this is ED.
                  (beat)
        LEENA!

                    LEENA
        I want any and all information you
        can dig up over the next few
        weeks on this case.

                ED WILLIAMS
        Look, LEENA, the guy is
        deranged. That's all. Didn't you
        read his psych profile?

LEENA
Yes, but I want to know what really happened to him. The media account that we've all read is their story. Now, I want his full story told. I know that something terrible happened to him. Find it.

ED WILLIAMS
Nothing happened to him! He's deranged!

LEENA
But, there's more to this case. I want you to talk to friends, neighbors, anybody living in his life. Mirror profile him.

ED WILLIAMS
Mirror profile him?

LEENA
Yes! We know he grew up without a father, so seek out a young man of his age with the same experience.

ED WILLIAMS
And, just what would constitute the same life experience as TIM OLSON's.

LEENA
We know he adored his father; find how the sole custody affected him etc., etc.

ED WILLIAMS
Alright.

LEENA
Go to the Dual Parenthood Conference and interview anyone who will talk to you.

ED WILLIAMS
Alright, I'll do that and get back to you. Meanwhile, when am I getting paid? You still owe me for the Newton case.

LEENA
I sent you $10,000. It should be in your account sometime today.

CUT TO:
INT. CONFERENCE ROOM 2 - DAY

JACOB
When my brother's dad came around, this kind of left a hole in me. It's like, why am I different? Why am I the only one that

doesn't have a dad? I wanted to know about him. I wanted to know who he was, where he was, what he did, just everything. Why didn't he want me? Why did my mom not want him to want me? It's just a kind of feeling like he could make things better. That he could turn around this whole mess that was going on at home. That he was going to be some guy that rode up and took me away from everything that was happening to me at home. I don't really know how I should feel about it, or what I was feeling about it. You know, it's just the persistent anger that sort of leads to the "I'll show you" kind of attitude. You wanna beat me, I'll give you a reason to beat me. And then as I got older, you wanna hit me, I'll hit you back. That's when the little beatings turned into brawls. People would be holding people down and back. Any chance we got, we would throw punches at one another. This led to my step dad being arrested for fighting with us. This led to all kinds of problems. I started hooking out of school. I started dabbling with drugs and alcohol. We never had any money, so for some quick cash, I sold a little bit of drugs. Nothing major, just small time stuff, but it put a few bucks in my pocket. I'd be away from home for days. I would just not show up and nobody really cared if you came home or not. My brother and I talk about it now. We could have just disappeared and nobody would have cared.

CUT TO:
INT. DPI CONFERENCE - DAY

JEAN OSBORNE, a sixty-something year-old grandmother, is at the podium speaking.

                JEAN OSBORNE

My name is JEAN OSBORNE. I'm from Bluffton, Indiana, and I'm a grandmother. I came to this conference on dual parenting to share some points of view of where we've been, keeping in touch. How we've been trying to provide an extended family to a child and validate our rights as grandparents. Our little granddaughter was born in 1989.

Her parents had problems, and we tried to be supportive in addressing those problems. We helped with housing, medical bills, babysitting, and anything to get this little child going. She had extensive medical problems. We became bonded to her and provided her with many things, including medical care, nurturance, and opportunities. Our daughter had used drugs as a teenager, and she returned to using drugs again after the birth of our granddaughter. This led to her getting a divorce. Shortly after, she terminated all communications with us. She obtained a protective order to keep us from seeing the child. I'm sure our granddaughter, having lived in our home for five years, is devastated, and we're devastated. We've spent an awful lot of money in attorney's fees, but nothing has changed.

CUT TO:
EXT. A BUSY TWO LANE STREET- DAY

We follow MR. B's SUV as he drives down the street

Forced Absence / 30

and makes a turn into his martial arts studio's parking lot. He gets out of the car, goes to the front door, opens the front door, and goes inside.

CUT TO:
INT. MARTIAL ARTS STUDIO - DAY

MR. B is sitting on a stool. The song "TAKE IT AWAY" by THE MIGHTY HELLBENDERZ is playing in the background.

              TAKE IT AWAY

Too quick to cut me. You went straight for the throat
It's a woman's prerogative. I swell a yellow turn coat
Made a promise to me in front of God and our friends
Let's call it a day; this is where it ends, where it ends
Just take it away, take it away
Oh, I can't believe it's all over now
They can take it away, they can take it all somehow
Take it away

                 MR. B
       After our first child was born, my
       ex-wife had a very severe case of
       post-partum depression. I had to
       take care of our son because she
       just couldn't. Now, after the
       second child was born, my ex-wife
       went through a lot of physical
       changes, and she felt bad about
       her chest area and her stomach

area. She started to slip into her post-partum depression again. But this time, she handled it a lot better. However, because she was used to me taking care of the first child, she pretty much demanded that I take care of this one. When I left for work, she would step up to the plate. She took care of the kids during the day. In the evenings and on the weekends when I'd come home, she would complain and bitch all day: "These kids are too much for me. It's too hard here. It's difficult raising these kids. You just don't understand because you're out working a job, talking to people. I don't get that. I don't get that communication with another person. So, me and my sisters are going out." After hours of this, she would leave. So, here I am with a two year old and a brand new baby. I'm alone on the weekend, raising them, while my wife's at the bar with her sisters. It started with once in a month. Next thing I know, it's every other week. Then, it's every week. It got to a point where I was concerned. Why did she need to go out that much? On the nights that I could afford and find a babysitter, I would go out with them. They'd be having a good time. They'd be dancing and drinking. I'd have maybe two, three drinks and then I'd watch her. (more)

TAKE IT AWAY (Contd.)
Pay attention young man, you'll be paying indeed
With your love or your money. By the way, did you have any dreams?
Dreams with your children, dreams that don't end sad
Cause 500 feet the court said is as close as I get to be their dad
Just take it away, take it away
Oh, I can't believe it's all over now
They can take it away, they can take it all some how
Take it away, just take it away. Oh, just take it away
Oh, I can't believe. Just take it away
Just take it away (x2)

MR. B (cont.)
Four, five, six, eight drinks later, she would be just drunk. Wouldn't know what she was doing. She'd be hanging off of everybody. I'd have to carry her to the car. And when we got home, I'd have to

actually carry her physically inside the house. There were nights when she would wake up in the middle of the night, get out of bed, go over to the clothing's hamper, and pee in it thinking it was the bathroom; she would be that drunk. We left a Christmas party early because she was embarrassing me after having too much to drink. On the way home, she was stripping in the car, taking off everything. So by the time we got home, I had to redress her and carry her inside the house, past my mom who was mortified at the sight. There were times she would just throw up everywhere; she peed in the bed several times. It was very frustrating because I wanted her to have a good time, but she was past that good time point.

CUT TO:
INT. DPI CONFERENCE - DAY

> DR. NEILAND
> My name is MICHAEL NEILAND, I am a medical doctor. I am a practicing physician. I practice

dermatology and skin pathology. I was married to another physician whom I met during our training at the John Hopkins hospital, and we were married for about 15 years. We both had separate, but very busy, practices. In addition, we're both on the faculty of the University Of Pittsburgh School Of Medicine. Like so many couples, problems developed in our marriage. These problems had to do with communications, our respective value systems, and the handling of money. These were problems that neither of us was able to resolve. I wanted very much to sustain my marriage for everyone's sake, particularly for my three children. However, it was impossible to do so in a harmonious atmosphere, and I found that I really had no choice after a great deal of counseling sessions by a psychiatrist and a psychologist in which we both participated. It was impossible to resolve our problems, and I decided that the best course for me was to divorce my wife. I wanted very much to continue to have a close, loving relationship with my children who, at the time of the divorce, were about fifteen, seven, and six years of age. My goals were to share custody of my children 50 percent of the time, to provide a home for them, and to provide all the love and care that a father should give his children. I felt perfectly competent to do so. Prior to divorcing my wife, I sought legal counsel who made great efforts to try to resolve our problems one last time with my ex-wife's counsel. Unfortunately, this did not succeed. After I filed for divorce, we continued to live in the family home for a number of months while the attorneys discussed the disposition of property. I also hoped that the attorneys would come up with a reasonable schedule for the children. It was decided that I would stay in the family home and that my wife would have ample time to find another home. Once this was decided, I hoped we would go on to other issues such as how we would develop a schedule for the children to keep their lives running as harmoniously as possible, and try to divide the property that we have between us. A few months later, I was away at a medical meeting and returned to an empty house. My children were gone. A substantial portion of the family possessions were gone, if not the greater majority of them. Most of the furniture in the house was gone. All the toys that the children ever had were gone, including their beds and their bureaus. One would walk into that house and not feel that a child had ever lived in that home. At this point, I was devastated and totally taken by surprise. It had never occurred to me that in my absence, my wife would essentially clean out the house

CUT TO:
EXT. COURTHOUSE - DAY

We see the main facade of the courthouse adorned with several American flags and patriotic ribbons. On the foreground are the lunchtime crowd, cars, and pedestrians on the busy street and parking lot.

CUT TO:
INT. THE COURTROOM - DAY

> **JUDGE**
> MS. THOMPSON, your motion seeks to convert the death penalty sentence to time served.
>
> **LEENA**
> Yes, your honor.
>
> **JUDGE**
> This is highly unusual.
>
> **PROSECUTOR**
> And that's why the court should deny the motion "sua sponte." Lest we forget, the accused is a monster who massacred his own mother in cold blood.
>
> **LEENA**
> The rules of court allow a great deal of latitude in the couching of post-conviction motions in capital cases.
>
> **PROSECUTOR**
> Your Honor, this is an attempt to truncate the procedures for motion for a new trial. The defendant claims that the jury was

deprived of relevant information during the trial, but he's not asking for a new trial.

LEENA
The motion before the court is a matter of law. The opinion of the jury is irrelevant. In so far as the court has broad powers and discretion in disposing post-conviction motions, this court may open the judgment and nullify, modify, or leave it undisturbed at the conclusion of this hearing.

JUDGE
MS. THOMPSON, you're right. But, you've chosen a more perilous route for your client. I hope you're aware of this.

LEENA
Yes, your honor.

JUDGE
Very well then, you may proceed.

CUT TO:
INT. JAIL - ATTORNEY'S MEETING ROOM - DAY

LEENA
I want you to tell me everything

that happened to you after your dad and mom divorced.

TIM

Well . . .

FADE TO BLACK

DISSOLVE TO:
INT. THE COURTROOM - DAY

LEENA

In this State, when a minor commits a transgression, we hold the parents liable. If truants vandalize their neighbor's property, we hold the parents financially liable. There is a reason for that. Our laws mandate that parents, guardians, and adults exercise diligence, good judgment, and accountability. We want parents and guardians to teach their wards what constitutes acceptable behavior. After the child reaches the age of majority, we hold the child liable. Our justice system believes that the child has had 18 years of nurturing, training, and discipline by his parents. But, what happens if the State, through its

> irresponsible laws and corrupt judiciary, deprived the child full access to the love, bond, and nurture of the parent more able to give him the right upbringing? Is the child at fault?

CUT TO:
INT. JAIL - ATTORNEY'S MEETING ROOM - DAY

> TIM
> I remember that after the divorce, my mother used to always talk badly about my father. She would always call him bad names and everything. And, that's the thing too; she would never shut up about it. Always trying to brainwash me. Telling me how horrible he was. I guess that stuff works on her friends because they would always tell me the same thing. Who the hell are they? They didn't know him and never tried to get to know him.

BACK TO THE COURTROOM

> LEENA
> What if the developmental problems were brought before a

corrupt judge of the family court system and nothing was done.

PROSECUTOR
Objection.

JUDGE
What's your objection?

PROSECUTOR
Impugning the reputation of the court system and scandalous remarks.

JUDGE
Everybody knows that the family court system is not a stellar judiciary. They have problems. It's been all over the media. MS. THOMPSON's remarks are not directed at the criminal division. Objection is overruled. You may proceed.

LEENA
You have a state legislature that passes irresponsible laws based on how much bribery, disguised as campaign contributions, its members receive without careful consideration to the effect it might have on its residents. These

> irresponsible and biased laws are then turned over to corrupt, inefficient, malfeasant judges to enforce. This mix creates chaos in the lives of children who come in contact with the system. Granted, not all family court judges are corrupt. Some are too lazy to read the briefs and the supporting documents. Some are sexist and biased for political expediency. And, the good judges are too overworked to manage the hundreds of cases before them. They're forced to rely extensively on law clerks and paralegals to craft opinions that are grounded neither on facts, nor precedential case laws but on sympathy and personal biases. The courts should spend more time uniting families and less time keeping them apart. PROFESSOR HARTMAN's research may enlighten the court.

CUT TO:
INT. DPI CONFERENCE - DAY

> PROF. HARTMAN
> The United States Supreme Court,

however, has circumscribed the scope of fundamental liberty rights by reserving the matters of family intimate decision making. Most notable, the rearing and bearing of children. The court, in a case called Lassiter vs. Department of Social Services, further found that this protected ambit of constitutional safeguards includes a parent's right for the comfort, care, and nurturance of one's child. The U.S. Supreme Court has discerned that fundamental liberty rights are those rights that are rooted in this nation's history and tradition, and are those rights found in the ordered concept of liberty and that if the states want to restrict these rights, the onus is on the states. It's a higher burden of proof, in other words, to show that it has a compelling interest that is narrowly tailored to the legislative goals that are sought to be accomplished. In practical effect, what that usually means is that the exercise of liberty rights ultimately prevails. That's why they're so significant.

CUT TO:
INT. THE COURTROOM - DAY

                LEENA
These judges think that they can ruin the lives of these non-custodial parents without consequence. How wrong could they be? If my client is a monster, then this monster has the state and the family court judges to thank for his existence.

CUT TO:
INT. DPI CONFERENCE - DAY

                DR. HOWLAND
Now, another stage is anger. Anger is a very common aspect of the divorce situation for many of the reasons that I've mentioned earlier. Anger and hostility can also be viewed as a coping mechanism for many individuals. Deep down, they feel guilty and inadequate that their marriage failed. Anger may also be a way of lashing out and protecting themselves from feelings of guilt and being inadequate. On the other hand, anger can also be

used as a form of punishment as one may view the divorce, and what happened in the relationship, as being unfair and that individuals may need to be punished. Unfortunately, anger can really spread out to other individuals. Anger is usually expressed toward oneself, but also children, friends, family members, etc. All of these could be the recipients of a lot of anger and hostility.

CUT TO:
INT. JAIL - ATTORNEY'S MEETING ROOM - DAY

TIM
I remember this one day came. She had taken all his clothes, computers, his whole business files, and ...

CUT TO:
EXT. CARMICHAEL COMPOUND - DAY

Jane and her three children (young TIM and his two SISTERS) drag two garbage bags full of men's clothes out on the back yard. Flames are shooting out of a nearby bonfire. A few yards away, next to a file cabinet, are piles of men's suits, shoes, briefcases, computers, and foot lockers.

> JANE
> Kids, take all your daddy's clothes out of the bags and scatter them all over the lawn so he can see them.

The daughters help their mother, but young Tim sits on a nearby footlocker instead.

> DAUGHTER
> Will Daddy be mad if he sees his clothes on the ground?

> JANE
> No! He'll be happy just to have some of his clothes back.

Jane grabs some of his suits, removes them from their hangers, and throws them in the fire.

> JANE
> Look what you've done to this family. Damn you!

She is consumed by an uncontrollable rage which she's trying to vent by pacing erratically in the yard and sobbing. A few seconds later, she refocuses her attention on destroying her husband's belongings. Jane and her daughters feed more business papers into the flames. She carries a desktop computer and stands in front of the fire while she admonishes him:

> JANE
> How can you do this to me? How can you do this to your children? We loved you! We supported you! We did everything for you. And, this is how you repay us! Well, this is how I repay you!

She throws his computer in the fire. The girls watch as the flame consumes their father's belongings.

> JANE
> Wait a minute! Stop! I have a better idea.

She grabs some of the clothes and throws them in the fire. She motions for the kids to follow her lead. The girls respond positively while young Tim is mortified by the venomous rant anchoring the destruction of his dad's belongings. He sits on a foot locker, his lips and fingers quivering. His mother confronts him:

> JANE
> (To the boy)
> Are you going to work, or sit there and whine all day like that no good daddy of yours?

The boy starts to sob. She sees him crying, but ignores him anyway. She takes another heap of files from the cabinet and dumps them in the fire. She goes to the boy sitting on one of the many foot lockers. Disappointed that young Tim seems to be more sympathetic to his father's plight than hers, she stares at him quizzically.

YOUNG TIM
Mom, why are you doing this?
First, you make us tell all those lies
to the judge. Then, you gave all
his good clothes to the Salvation
Army. Now, you're burning all his
business papers and messing up
his few remaining clothes.

JANE
(scoffing)
You need to quit crying like a
sissy.

She goes to the foot locker that he's sitting on, snatches the keyboard, and tugs on the cable.

JANE
Move! Get up! Get up!

She throws the keyboard and some files in the burning pile. The two daughters stop and stare pensively at their sobbing brother. Jane sees the girls, pauses, and rolls her eyes. Reluctantly, she goes to TIM and squats next to him.

                    JANE
When we're done, we'll go get
some pizza.

She tries to embrace him, but the boy pushes her back.

                    YOUNG TIM
Don't touch me! I hate you!

We follow the boy as he runs into the house.

CUT TO:
INT. JAIL - ATTORNEY'S MEETING ROOM - DAY

                    TIM
This was after she told the judge
that my dad had removed all his
things from the house. Although
my dad denied it, somehow the
judge believed her lies instead.

CUT TO:
INT. DPI CONFERENCE - DAY

                    RADFER
And now, there is anger, agony,

and pain. Now, he has to judge and rate his relationship with his parents and score them. The scores for both sides are very low. This deteriorates his self-esteem. To a child, having a nice family contributes immensely to his self-esteem. Giving low or negative scores to his parents results in the child's low esteem which affects his self-confidence and invariably lowers his self-reliance.

BACK TO THE COURTROOM

           LEENA
Every year, millions of Americans seek to end their marriages. Some follow the normal channels, while others choose a more radical approach.

FADE IN

CUT TO:
INT. DPI CONFERENCE - DAY

           KOPP
My wife called 911 while I was in the home; the only thing that transpired was that we had an argument. When the police came,

she alleged that I physically
abused her, which was false.

CUT TO:
INT. PSYCHOLOGIST'S OFFICE - DAY

>					JEFF
> They're usually the first line of defense in the divorces. Often, if there are children involved, the first thing that usually happens is a claim of some type of alleged abuse going on by one parent. It is often used as a strategy for sympathy at the hearing and for achieving certain objectives that otherwise would elude them. Don't get me wrong, there are men and women that physically and emotionally abuse their spouses and they deserve to be condemned and penalized. However, the rising number of false claims of abuse unfortunately demands that some caution be exercised when claims of abuse are first made during divorce or child custody proceedings. As I was saying, we just had a case of the gentlemen

that was accused of showing his four or five year-old son some pornographic images on the Internet. Now, I'm not saying that he did or didn't. But, immediately after making the allegation, the wife changed the locks on the house and kicked the husband out the door. There was no evidence presented, no police report or investigations, and no conviction. She insisted that the only reason for this was that "he showed my four year old pornography."

CUT TO:
INT. DPI CONFERENCE - DAY

          KOPP

On December 2 of that same year, the police showed up again, escorting me and my father out of the home because my wife and my children were not there. They had left for the weekend. And, this was a total shock to me. I didn't think it would come to this. I was told to leave the home, which is our home where we had our children, and I had no place to go. It was very scary to know that you can be ordered to leave your home based on lies and false allegations. Nothing has been proven, and there could not be evidence because nothing happened. But, still the court system gave credence to her allegations and that was enough to have me forced out of our home.

CUT TO:
INT. PSYCHOLOGIST'S OFFICE - DAY

> ED WILLIAMS
> So, you have seen these orders used as tactics or weapons?

> JEFF
> Yeah, as tactics in the courts' hearings in child custody battles. The first response, a lot of times, is that a child is being physically abused or a child's not being treated right or whatever is going on that's wrong or criminal. Men are too often reluctant to admit that their wives abuse them. So, the majority of the time, the wives accuse the husbands of abusing them even though there's no history. By going to an emergency

room for proof, there's no medical care done that can be filed as evidence.

ED WILLIAMS
So, the spouses get kicked out of their homes, or what?

JEFF
Yeah! What generally happens is that. This is the way to get the accused out of the house through the use of protections for abuse orders (PFA). Without the grounds of the abuse charges, you don't have grounds for an order, a PFA. If I want you to stay 500 feet away from me, I have to have an excuse. I can't go to court and say, "I just want a PFA." They're not going to give it to me. If I go to court and say, "I want one because I want him out of the house", "I want him away from me", "I want him away from the kids," when they ask for a reason, I have to say something happened. I can't just ask for a PFA because I feel like it, ok? I have to have justification for it. And, what better justification can you have other than I've been

abused?

>   ED WILLIAMS
> Is there any fact checking before enforcing these PFAs?

>   JEFF
> No, just the allegations. And, you may find out later during later court hearings that there wasn't any credible basis for the PFA. Even if there was abuse, there may not be sufficient grounds for legal charges, or there may not even be any charges whatsoever. Like I said, if there's been no history, you would assume that if I've had my nose broken, my jaw broken, and black and blue, I'm gonna have photographs. I'm gonna call the police because they can take photos. It doesn't happen, so for nine out of ten, the information or proof isn't there, but they still allege abuse, cause without it, you can't get the PFA.

CUT TO:
INT. CONFERENCE ROOM 3 - DAY

>   JIM
> I was told that I assaulted my ex-

wife with a door; my ex-wife has a black belt in judo, a brown belt in karate, and was on the Olympic team in 1980. I consider her an expert in martial arts.

CUT TO:
INT. MARTIAL ARTS STUDIO

> MR. B
> She made life very difficult for me because she felt so inadequate about herself. We'd be walking down the street and if she saw a nice looking woman go by she'd yell at me: "why are you looking at her?" Even though I might not have even seen her, I still got the full dress down about the girl. It got so bad that I was forced to go through supermarket aisles with my head down and I couldn't look at magazines, lest I see women in them. She tried to control every aspect of my life. That's when she started controlling my body, making me walk through aisles with my head down, making me walk in broad daylight with my head down so I wouldn't look at women. It got to the point where

she insisted on previewing movies before I could watch them to ascertain that they had no nude scenes in them. That was how insecure she felt, and I gave in to her demands, hoping to help her through her problems. After four years of this, I started resisting. I was just tired of the life of hell that she was putting me through. Knowing that I had never cheated on her made her behavior even more perplexing. I kept asking, what did I do wrong? Where did I go wrong? Why is she making me do this?

CUT TO:
INT. CONFERENCE ROOM 3 - DAY

                JIM

In fact, when I filed for custody so that I could have better visitation, that's when all hell broke loose. She filed charges of assault against me, which never happened. How do you throw a door into somebody's face that opens in on them and is totally locked? How do you throw a door into somebody's face when you ring the doorbell and step back ten feet because you're afraid of what they'll do to you because they have the skills and all you want are your children?

CUT TO:
INT. MARTIAL ARTS STUDIO

          MR. B

She would smack me on the face and challenge me to fight her. Shouting, "Come on! You call yourself a man? If you were a man, then you would be able to hit me." And, she'd do this repetitively. I'm not talking just little 5 or 10 minute fights, I'm talking hours. How many hours am I talking about? I would come home from work at about 6:00 p.m., we would eat supper, and if something wasn't put away right, she'd start from then on and she wouldn't stop. There were times when by 2:00 a.m., the fight would be still going on. She would be insisting that I hit her. Shouting, "Hit me! Hit me! Hit me!" until she finally realized that I was not going to hit her. I don't know of too many men disciplined enough to resist the temptation to fight back. Some people have very low tolerance. I credit my martial arts training for my high tolerance. Through my training in Tae kwon do, I am able to control my anger, control my actions, and control everything I do. If it wasn't for that, I would have hit her and probably inflicted very severe injuries on her. She was a very annoying person that enjoyed pushing everybody around. She pushed them, made sure they stay down, and didn't come back up. And, when she did that to me, she took it a step further by slapping me, hitting, and kicking me. One evening, we went to a function with some of our friends at a bar. My wife said she was going to order another round of drinks for us. Moments later, two of our friends sitting across from me were wide eyed, jaws dropping, and prodding me to turn around. I turned around and saw my wife making out with one guy while she was reaching down into the pants of the other guy and fondling his genitals. That was my breaking point. I walked up to her, pulled her off the guys and said, "if this is what you want, fine so be it." Then, I pushed her back toward them. And, I still never hit her. Did it hurt? Yes, it enraged me, but thankfully, her whole tactics to get me to hit her never worked. Hitting her would have put me, put me in an unpleasant situation because I'd probably, in all likelihood, be in prison now.

CUT TO:
INT. PSYCHOLOGIST'S OFFICE - DAY

ED WILLIAMS
Have you had any experience with false allegations on custody cases?

JEFF
Yes, quite a bit.

ED WILLIAMS
Could you talk about some of those cases? Abuse, sexual abuse, inappropriate behavior of some type, drug and . . .

JEFF
In questionable custody cases, one

parent usually accuses the other of drug addiction, violence toward the child, or some antisocial behavior. It's hard to prove this against the spouse because there has to be medical records or physical evidence there. But, if the sexual abuse allegations are substantiated or evidence of drug abuse against the individual exists, then he or she is an unfit parent that should not have custody.

ED WILLIAMS
So, is there any hope for a parent who has been a victim of false allegations in pursuing custody of his or her child?

JEFF
I think they can still pursue custody ok. Some courts have been inundated with too many false allegations in the past that some judges are skeptical of claims made after the relationships have ended. But, it's very hard to overcome this type of allegation. It depends on the judge. It depends on your attorney. And, again, it depends

> on the economic resources that
> the accused has to defend himself
> and fight for the custody. In a lot
> of cases, if you don't have the
> economic resources, you're pretty
> much stuck. You don't get
> custody, and you get supervised
> visitation, if anything at all.

BACK TO THE COURTROOM

> LEENA
> If you think for a minute that this
> happens only to married men,
> think again.

CUT TO:
EXT. ALBERT'S HOUSE - DAY

A deputy sheriff in an unmarked car pulls up in front of a house. He alights from the car and goes to the front door on which he pounds. A man in his underwear opens the door.

> DEPUTY SHERIFF
> Are you ALBERT CUNNINGHAM?

> ALBERT
> Yes.

The deputy hands over a legal document to

CUNNINGHAM.

> DEPUTY SHERIFF
> MR. CUNNINGHAM, you've been served. You have 20 minutes to take your belongings and leave the house.

> ALBERT
> Why? This is my home. It's all paid for. No mortgage of any kind. Even the taxes are current.

> DEPUTY SHERIFF
> MR. CUNNINGHAM, read the papers. That is a PFA. Protection From Abuse order. Your wife filed a petition against you.

> ALBERT
> Wife! I don't have a wife.

> DEPUTY SHERIFF
> Well then, your girlfriend.

ALBERT opens the documents and glances at the second page.

> ALBERT
> Becky! I'll be damned if imma' let that slut steal my house from me. I caught the bitch cheating, and

asked her to get out of my house. Now, I'm being kicked out my house. I bought this house before I ever met the whore. How the fuck can this shit happen?

DEPUTY SHERIFF
She went before a judge and swore that she's afraid of being physically abused by you.

ALBERT
Abuse her. I have never abused her and would never.

DEPUTY SHERIFF
MR. CUNNINGHAM, I think that you need to call your attorney. But, for now, you have 15 minutes to leave the house with your belongings.

ALBERT
15 minutes. I own everything in the mother fucking house. How do you expect me to take all these out of here in 15 minutes?

DEPUTY SHERIFF
MR. CUNNINGHAM, I really don't care what you take or leave behind. I'm here only to enforce

the court order.

                    ALBERT
And, if I don't leave?

                DEPUTY SHERIFF
You have no choice sir. If you don't leave, you'll be arrested and jailed.

                    ALBERT
15 minutes? I need more than 15 minutes to take a shower and get dressed.

                DEPUTY SHERIFF
                (Motioning for him to go in)
You're wasting time.

The two walk into the house.

DISSOLVE TO:
EXT. ALBERT'S PORCH - DAY

ALBERT comes out of the house escorted by the DEPUTY SHERIFF. ALBERT is carrying his briefcase and a couple of items of clothing which he throws in his car and then drives away. The DEPUTY locks the door and drives off.

CUT TO:
INT. CLUB/RESTAURANT - EVENING

ANDREA and ED WILLIAMS are at a table in the restaurant. ED takes a sip from his cocktail. ANDREA sobs silently for a few moments while ED waits patiently for her to continue with her story. ANDREA collects herself, takes a sip from her wine glass, and continues. The song "WHAT AM I SUPPOSED TO DO?" by THE MIGHTY HELLBENDERZ BAND is playing in the background.

WHAT AM I SUPPOSED TO DO?
The birds and the bees, they sing so loud
I found me a girl, gonna make you proud
Just a few questions that I have in store
I'm sure in a minute, I'll have some more

Now, she's the best thing in my life
And I hope someday to make her my wife
This emotion is so new
But dad, what am I supposed to do

                ANDREA
    My ex and his team of attorneys
    have no conscience. Neither does
    the judge. They see me on the
    ground, lying face down, all
    bloodied up, and they keep
    stomping on me. Damn! What
    kind of people are these?

ED nods.

ANDREA
The judge sits there and gives them everything they ask for. I am paying more than sixty percent of my income in child support. Not that my ex-husband needs the money mind you, but as a punitive exercise. Now, he just filed another motion to jack up my support payments. I am too broke to afford good attorneys. My utilities are about to be shut off. My car payments are lagging. Yet, he wants more money. Where is the justice? Where are the ethics, fairness, and morality in the court system?
(Beat)
Let me show you something.

ANDREA opens her purse and takes out a dollar bill. She shoves it at ED WILLIAMS.

WHAT AM I SUPPOSED TO DO?
(cont.)
Said let's take a walk and I'll try my best
If you're happy inside, then forget about the rest
So, he turned and smiled like never before
And said, please, please Dad, would you tell me some more

Cause if she gets ugly and you get fat
Ain't nothing much wrong with that
As long as you love her till the very end
She'll be your confidant and your best friend

> ANDREA
> What does it say right there in the middle, right above the one?

ED looks at the currency.

> ED WILLIAMS
> In God We Trust.

> ANDREA
> (Nodding)
> Yes, In God we Trust. When you appear in court, the first thing they do is tell you to place your hand on the bible and be sworn. We invoke the name of God while treating one another like shit. In the name of God, they take all the money of a non-custodial parent about to be evicted from her apartment and give it to her ex living in a mansion.

> ED WILLIAMS
> Do you blame the judge for your current predicament?

WHAT AM I SUPPOSED TO DO?
(cont.)
So, we walked and we talked down that old dirt road
I knew all those questions were a heavy load
But, he's my boy, and I'll make him proud
So, I answered him real loud

Son, if you like her and she likes you
Here is what you have to do
Get down on your knees and ask for her hand
Then shout it out loud, all over this land

ANDREA

You're damn right. I blame the judge. I blame the judge. I blame the legislature who passed these cockamamiec laws, and the governor who signed the damn bill into law. I blame them all. May they all burn in hell for what they've done to me.
(beat)
I'm a law-abiding citizen. Never been arrested before. Not a single parking ticket in my name. Shit, when the speed limit says 60 miles per hour, I do 57. What have I done to deserve all this harsh treatment? Absolutely nothing! Nothing!! Seeing what they've put

             me through. The embarrassment
             of eating peanut butter and jelly
             sandwiches every day at work
             instead of going out to restaurants
             with my friend. The constant fear
             of being thrown in jail by a judge
             who threatened to do just that if
             I'm unable to pay my ex.

                        ED WILLIAMS
             What do you mean?

                        ANDREA
             What do I mean?

ED's cell phone rings a couple of times. He fetches it from his jacket.

                        ED WILLIAMS
             Sorry, I have to take this.

He answers the phone.

                        ED WILLIAMS
             Williams Investigations.
                        (Beat)
             Congratulations, LEENA. This is
             great news indeed. You're
             welcome.
                        (Beat)
             You can thank me with a check.

> (Beat)
> I am meeting with her now.
> (Beat)
> Bye.

He puts the phone back in his pocket.

> **ANDREA**
> Looks like you won the case.

> **ED WILLIAMS**
> This was particularly nasty and complex one, but we won.

CUT TO:
INT. CONFERENCE ROOM 3 - DAY

> **JIM**
> She wanted the business so that she could have an income and medical benefits. She told me that if she got the business, she would have her attorney throw out the alimony papers. It would be easier for the children. So, I gave it to her. I gave her my only source of income and left the marriage with nothing. She got the house, the best car, the money making for the house, and the cars - the business. And, she got my kids.

CUT TO:
INT. DPI CONFERENCE - DAY

> **KOPP**
> I've been paying 1400 dollars a month for child support which works out to about 50 percent of my gross annual income. And, this is also a very difficult task to deal with because it puts severe financial strain on me. And, my wife will end up with the house that we worked together for over the last 15 years.

BACK TO THE COURTROOM

> **LEENA**
> $1400 per month in child support without accountability. Millions of families make less than that every month. What are these kids eating? Should the child eat lobster and filet mignon every day while the father lives in his car? Shouldn't the custodial parent pay half of the costs? The corrupt family court judges often use excessive unaffordable child support payments as a way of

keeping the non-custodial parent from seeing their children. Quite often, the defaulting parent goes underground.

CUT TO:
INT. MARTIAL ARTS STUDIO

> MR. B
> At that time, I believe that the child support was set at 1,000 some odd dollars per month. So, that's 500 bucks every paycheck. They also attached an extra 50 dollars for arrears. So, they were taking 55 percent of my income, which only left me with 400 in my paycheck. I was paying 315 dollars for the mortgage, my electric was 150, and the gas for my vehicle was like 80 dollars to get back and forth to work. By the time I was done, I didn't have any money for food, any money to treat my kids out on special occasions, or any money to basically pay any of my other bills. I had to sacrifice a little; I went six months with no electric in my house just so I could keep my house because I wasn't able to afford it.

CUT TO:
INT. CONFERENCE ROOM 3 - DAY

> JIM
> I felt like I was pushed out of my own house and the only way I could salvage what was left of my life was to leave the marriage, to leave my children, to leave my business, and to leave my way of life.

CUT TO:
INT. MARTIAL ARTS STUDIO

> MR. B
> She took her time and planned everything out thoroughly before filing for divorce. A year before filing for divorce, she insisted that all the installment accounts be in my name only. She took her name off the credit cards and mortgage. She drove me into bankruptcy before filing for divorce.

CUT TO:
INT. CONFERENCE ROOM 3 - DAY

                    JIM
          I went and lived with my parents
          because I couldn't afford to do
          anything else. Child support and
          alimony and everything else was
          just too much for me to be
          burdened with to even be actually
          able to consider living on my own.

CUT TO:
INT. DPI CONFERENCE - DAY

                    DR. NEILAND
          The children were initially
          reluctant to come back to my
          home because there was nothing
          there for them. Their beds were
          gone. All their toys were gone.
          And, the house did not look like a
          home anymore.

CUT TO:
INT. MARTIAL ARTS STUDIO

                    MR. B
          When we were in a conference
          with court personnel at Domestic
          Relations, she came there with
          some documents for me to sign.
          They included a list of properties
          that she wanted. Anything that we

owed money on, she left with me. She took only what we owned free and clear. She essentially took all the equity and left the debts behind.

CUT TO:
INT. DPI CONFERENCE - DAY

> DR. NEILAND
> It took me a number of months before I was able to make the house a place where the children had a certain comfort level in terms of toys and beds and so forth and so on.

CUT TO:
INT. MARTIAL ARTS STUDIO

> MR. B
> How fair is that? For her to just go in, help yourself to whatever she wants that's paid off, and leave me with none of that and now, I'm paying for the house, the cars, and stuff. And now, I've got to get out and buy new beds, buy microwaves, buy this and buy that, and I had to do it. I actually had to get hand me downs from

the neighbors for couches and beds so my kids had some place to sleep when they came over. She went to an apartment that was furnished with everything, but she still took all the stuff in the house. She took everything and left me nothing.

CUT TO:
INT. CONFERENCE ROOM 3 - DAY

                JIM

I pay over 1100 dollars a month for child care, or for child support, and currently another 300 dollars a month for child care cost. But, I still don't get to see my kids. I'm not a deadbeat dad. I'm a beaten dead dad. And, it hurts because I don't get to see my kids.

CUT TO:
INT. CLUB/RESTAURANT - EVENING

              ANDREA

When I got laid off, my unemployment benefits kicked in, but my benefits were less than my support payments. So, I had to borrow money to avoid going to jail. I keep asking myself, what

> crime have I committed to deserve all this bullshit? When Hollywood starlets drive under the influence, the judges tell them to do a public service announcement. When Wall Street executives commit a crime, they get probation. So, what makes me so bad that I need to be worried about going to jail? Nothing!

CUT TO:
INT. MARTIAL ARTS STUDIO

> MR. B
> I was selling kitchens (cabinets, fixtures, etc.) through a distributor and basically they told me my salary would be x amount. After working there for almost a year, due to bad economic condition, the company cut my salary from 1,200 dollars plus commissions to 300 dollars a month plus commission because no one was buying anything. So, my current wife and I went to my ex-wife and told her what happened, hoping that she'd understand. I was paying child support on time and everything was going good and this time, my current wife was

pregnant with her first child after being told that she would never be able to have kids. Now, pretty much in the wink of an eye, my pay got wiped out. So, I asked my ex-wife for help and pretty much she told us that she'd help. After a month and a half, I got a letter in the mail saying I had another court date for non-payment of child support. It had only been a month and a half and I was already 2,000 dollars in arrears? I was like, "I'll go to court and explain my situation to Judge Dobson." My current wife is getting stressed out because she thought everything was gonna be ok because the ex-wife said so. But, now she's pushing papers to basically get the money (that she knew that I didn't have) or throw me in jail for contempt of court. Under the law, I was entitled to a drastic reduction in my support obligations since the reduction in income was due to a change in circumstances not caused by me. The date came, I was there in the court room sitting by myself, and my ex-wife was on the other side sitting by her attorney. Judge Dobson was sitting up there, smacking his gavel one after another, boom, boom, and it's just like a production line. I was like, how could somebody make a judgment so quickly and just push everything through as he's doing? Pretty much, I got the answer because in the next couple minutes, I was up in front of him, and here I am, a father who gets his kids every weekend, and paying child support. I'd been honest with the system. Now, I'm in front of this judge and the only thing he could say to me was, "Are you in arrears?" "Yes," I said. "Do you have the 2000 dollars?" "Well, no sir," I replied. "Well, then you have 30 days to come up with the 2000 dollars to pay, or you're in jail." "How could I do that?" I retorted. He replied, "What do your kids mean to you?" I said they mean everything to me. He said, "Then you must find a way to move the heavens and the earth to support your children." Now, keep in mind, I just don't support my children, I support two households: the one I'm living in now and my ex-wife's. With a salary of 300 dollars, there's no way to come up with 2000 dollars.

CUT TO:
INT. CLUB/RESTAURANT - EVENING

              ANDREA

My ex and I ended our marriage and we couldn't agree on the terms. We came to court looking for an impartial sympathetic judge to help us sort things out. Instead, we got this power hungry prick who thinks he's some sort of demigod. And from what I've heard, a lot of these family court judges and domestic relations judges, or whatever they call themselves, are like that. They treat non-custodial parents like shit. They look down on us with no respect, no empathy, no justice, and no humanity.

CUT TO:
INT. MARTIAL ARTS STUDIO

              MR. B

And, the thing that really confuses me about the court system, till today, is why did he have to be that way? It just felt like he didn't want to take the time. Like, he was there for a paycheck. Here I go: guilty, not guilty, guilty, not guilty. Whatever he decided. You know, maybe the person was wearing red and he didn't like the color red: he's guilty. I really don't know how he made the judgment. I think it was dishonest, I really do, because for a man of his stature being a judge, he is altering people's lives, their outcome, their professions, their livelihood, are all at his fingertips. You have some people unable to work due to illness, accidents, plant closures, etc. Yet, this judge didn't conduct any hearing whatsoever. The right to a hearing is a constitutional right of everybody. This judge did not accord any of the defendants opportunity to present their defenses in his "court." He skipped the mandatory hearing and goes straight to the sentencing phase. Everybody tells me, "oh well, but you can appeal it." Of course you can, if you have 4000 dollars, because that's how much it would take to hire an attorney. All the ones that I called wanted 4000 dollars or more to take my case. I don't see why it takes $4000 to appeal a $2000 judgment. If I don't have $2000, how can I afford $4000? If I disagree with the judge's ruling, I should be able to appeal it without having to worry about the cost. The state should make it possible. And, that's why I think the system is screwing up. When you lock up people who can't pay through no fault of their own, what good does that do? At the end of their sentence, the ex-spouse and the kids still don't have the money, and the state has wasted thousands of dollars locking up people that it shouldn't. I think if the Dobsons of the court systems would just take the time to give each case a thorough hearing, so that instead of pushing through 50 or more cases in a day, maybe just push through ten, justice would be better served. Does that mean that the system might get backed up? Yeah, it does. At least the defendants will

> feel like they had their day in court and justice was done. There are a lot of non-custodial parents going before these judges that would do anything for their children. Anything. They love their kids just like I love mine, and it upsets me that there's a judge sitting on a bench right now that doesn't care. He really doesn't care; I mean it.

CUT TO:
INT. CONFERENCE ROOM 3 - DAY

> JIM
> The child care costs that I pay support the nanny that my ex-wife has to watch the kids because she can't. When I filed for custody, one of the first things out of my mouth in the courtroom was, "I want to care for my kids." I moved from 45 minutes away to within five blocks. I moved to the same school system because I wanted to be involved with my kids, because I want to care for them. I can't care for them, I don't get to see them, and it's just not fair for them growing up without a father, nor is it fair for me to be forced to

pay monies for things that I wanted to do myself. Caring for my kids was something important to me. As a parent, I feel that it's my responsibility, not somebody else's who you buy and pay to take care of your children. When the divorce finally came through after two and half years, I was told at the divorce table that I could see my kids whenever I wanted, all I needed to do was call. That wasn't written into the divorce decree. It was put into an agreement between my attorney, her attorney, and my ex-wife and me. That agreement was never carried through. That agreement was never allowed to come to fruition. The only thing that was put into writing was visitation once a week, every other weekend. I understand now that that's standard for getting dad out of the way, for getting dad to pay.

BACK TO THE COURTROOM

LEENA
Most non-custodial parents already impoverished by

> exorbitant child support levies stay and fight. They fight for visitation. They fight for joint custody. They fight, fight, and fight to be treated as parents. Like racehorses with blinders, the corrupt judges ignore their pleas. They try to justify their irrationality by ordering psychological evaluations. How dare non-custodial parents ask for joint custody? How dare they ask the courts to treat them as parents? How dare they want to see their kids every week? We may have a psycho here! Call in the shrink, but hold the Prozac, for now.

CUT TO:
INT. CONFERENCE ROOM 3 - DAY

> JIM
> Last year, trying to get custody, or better unrestricted visitation rights, for me to see my children, I spent over 12,000 dollars in legal fees. Legal fees, psychological profile, evaluations, custody evaluations that didn't get to come to fruition, even though the

court ordered them. Actions that, although the court ordered them for me on my behalf, I can't get; aren't enforceable. Even though it's on the books in the state of Pennsylvania, all the filings, all the motions, all the pleadings that my attorneys have presented on my behalf, showing that I am a responsible father and I want to be responsible for my children and have access to them, don't mean anything more than the paper they're printed on. There is no enforcement for court orders, for custody evaluation, or visitation rights for fathers, none at all.

BACK TO THE COURTROOM

                LEENA
The courts drag it on and on while ignoring the rights of children to bond with their natural parents.

CUT TO:
INT. DPI CONFERENCE - DAY

           SONG: I REMEMBER
Mom and Dad were hoping I was too young to remember
The cold words spoken during that empty December

Forced Absence / 88

Now, one was to miss every other baseball game
And the other's left out every other Sunday.
Ain't that a shame

Some say it's a puzzle
Some say it's a lie
But, I do remember being four or five
I don't remember the pictures in my mind
But, I do remember the feeling deep down inside
Like that puppy dog you had when you were just a kid
The one that had to go away to that nice farm to live

> DR. NEILAND
> It was my understanding that custody adjudication would not really take very much time. That it required interviews of the children, of the parents, perhaps some psychological testing and that it would take a number of weeks only. The custody adjudication went on for months. Finally, the following March of 1988, a report was presented to the court that recommended an equally shared custody arrangement. We attempted, and the court then scheduled, a hearing for the following June or July at which the psychologist

would testify, his report would be presented, and the custody arrangement would be established. The court recommended a custody arrangement of every other day, essentially, and every other weekend, except for the fact that my children hardly ever spent any time over night at my home. Things really deteriorated rapidly after that. My son always adhered to the custody schedule, but my daughter, who was six or seven at the time, started running away from my home inexplicably.
(More)

I REMEMBER
(cont.)

I had two sets of clothes, two sets of toys
Two sets of parents, two sets of heart ache covered with the joy
The toy stays here, you can play when you come back
Maybe for Christmas, you'll get another one for here and another at your Mother's

Some say it's a puzzle some, say it's a lie
But, I do remember being eight or nine
I don't remember the pictures in my mind

But, I do remember the feeling deep down inside
Like the neighbor that wouldn't let you play with her kids
Cause she didn't like your mama's boyfriend or his loud drunk rowdy friends

> DR. NEILAND
> (cont.)
> I was unable to get her to spend any time with me, and I appealed to the psychologist to let me know what was occurring that made my daughter run away from me. And, he told me that in his 30 years of experience, he had seen everything and would soon find out why my little girl was running away from me. I've never had any problems with any of my children. The psychologist unfortunately took many more months and never came up with a solution as to why my daughter kept running away, and on the advice of counsel, I filed a petition for contempt of court because my ex-wife felt I was not adhering to the custody schedule that required my daughter to spend certain amounts of time with me. There was a custody hearing on my

petition for contempt and at the hearing, the psychologist claimed that my daughter continued to run away from me because she was afraid of me. And, at the end of the custody hearing and contempt hearing which went on for 1100 pages of transcript and many hours and many dollars, the master, who had been appointed to hear the contempt petition, found my ex-spouse in contempt of court and then recommended that the psychologist be severed from the case and that yet another mental health professional should be appointed to find out if my daughter was afraid of me, and to continue to work with the family and try to solve this terrible problem in which I was not having any time with my youngest child. (More)

I REMEMBER
(cont.)

Does her boyfriend spend the night?
Does his new girlfriend feed you right?
You'll like mommy's new friend. He has a yacht
your daddy's gonna get you at six, he better not
forget

What's daddy's new girlfriend like? I don't know, but
Uncle Charlie says she's really, really hot

Some say it's a puzzle some, say it's a lie
But, I do remember being old enough not to cry
I do remember the pictures in my mind
And, I do remember those feelings deep down inside
Like your first love you were afraid to kiss
Or, that empty feeling the first time you weren't really missed
That empty feeling the first time you weren't really missed

                    DR. NEILAND
                      (cont.)

    Many more months went on and the psychiatrist, that both my ex-spouse and I chose, once again evaluated my daughter, evaluated me. We had endless sessions devoted to interviewing, and, very early on actually, the psychiatrist explained to me that the reason that my daughter was running away from me wasn't that she was afraid of me, but she was afraid of her mother's reaction if she spent any time with me, if she expressed any loving sentiment toward her father, and that the problem really was that my youngest child just was afraid of offending her mother. Well, another two years of this went on. The psychiatrist claimed that she was working with my daughter, working with my ex-spouse to lead her to understand that this was not in the best interest of my daughter, to be separated from her father.

BACK TO THE COURTROOM

          PROF. HARTMAN
And sadly, some parents use children as pawns in the bargaining process to gain concessions from former partners.

CUT TO:
INT. MARTIAL ARTS STUDIO

          MR. B
Before filing for divorce, while she's projecting all of this anger and hostility on me because of the way she feels about herself, she went to my mom, behind my back, and told her that if my mom didn't pay for her boob job and tummy tuck that she'd leave with

the kids and my mom would never see them again. This was very upsetting to my mom. Then on the other hand she talked to me like, "oh, I'm thinking about getting a boob job and tummy tuck so I can feel better about myself. That way you don't have to walk around with your head down and you can just watch the movies the way you want to and you don't have to worry about me not feeling good about myself." I thought, "Ok, this might be a turning point here." I'm all for it, because, frankly, I was tired of having to live my life that way. I thought that she was getting the money from her relatives. It was an extortion scheme and I didn't know. So, my ex-wife went and got the operation. Boob job and tummy tuck, everything went through with flying colors. Things got better for probably a month and then it got back to "normal" where she would say, "oh, put your head down", "don't look at that one", "don't look at this one", "don't do that", "don't do this." It became frustrating to me to where we began to fight more. I started to feel like I wasn't me! I had no control of my life; that it didn't matter what I did, what I said. I was worthless! And, to be honest, I think that was her goal, to make me feel that way, so she could control me easily. We'd fight about the issues of her drinking, going out, the boob job extortion, and walking through the aisles with my head down. I finally started to put my foot down and said, "listen, you told me that if you had this done, things would be all so much better and now, it's not. It's still the same old same old." I started to get fed up with everything and my love for her started to diminish, and then, I felt like I was just a toy and her puppet. When she was pregnant with the third child, she started advocating that we get an abortion. I didn't know why any wife would even suggest such a thing. After our separation, we went through marriage counseling. That was when it came out that after having our second child and getting the boob

job and tummy tuck, which my
mother paid for, she started
having affairs behind my back. So,
here she is cheating on me with
these guys and having affairs and
making my life miserable by
making me do those demeaning
things.

CUT TO:
INT. CONFERENCE ROOM 3 - DAY

                JIM

During the process of the custody
evaluation, and even prior to that,
my kids were used as pawns in this
area of family law called divorce.
They were constantly telling me
that I wasn't their dad because I
didn't live with them. Although
they did get to see me, I wasn't
really their dad. That was because
that was what their mom told
them.

           PROF. HARTMAN

Because even though best interest
is the current standard we use, I
think that to some extent it's a
very euphemistic standard and I
think, at times, can be at best,

fictional. That is to say we talk
about best interest standard, but
I'm not quite so sure and
comfortable that is in fact a child's
best interest that is always being
focused on.

BACK TO THE COURTROOM

> LEENA
> When the courts and the State stir
> things up by ignoring the notion of
> co-parenting but instead
> deliberate on primary parent, we
> have a prescription for acrimony.

CUT TO:
INT. DPI CONFERENCE - DAY

> HEIDISH
> And, that's the unfortunate thing
> that happens and has always
> happened in court related
> procedures; people demonizing
> and dehumanizing each other. To
> somebody who would just listen
> to these things, if you're just
> looking at the legal fights that go
> on, you'd wonder whether any of
> them could parent their child.
> You'd be thinking, how could
> anybody that bad be a good

parent? But in fact, it is kind of skewed. The attorneys are there to win your case, right? I mean, they're saying wonderful things about you and bad things about the other person. If you hired them, they would be doing the opposite; that's their job. This is part of the ugliness of our adversarial legal system.

CUT TO:
INT. THE COURTROOM - DAY

> LEENA
> In the seventies and eighties, several states enacted rules making it difficult for poor families to qualify for welfare. A woman had to get rid of her car, color TV, furniture, and husband or a live-in boyfriend. This resulted in a proliferation of households of women and children only. Many of these children with no father figures ended up in jails, accounting for explosion in crime rates and inmate population. As the state modified their welfare rules, the problem eased. In the nineties, the inequities within the

family court system came into focus. More and more children who were deprived of the love, bond, and nurture of both parents were ending up in jail, detention centers, and various forms of juvenile residential facilities. But, how does single parenting affect a young life, regardless the cause?

CUT TO:
INT. DPI CONFERENCE - DAY

> DR. RADFER
> The more conflict the child is exposed to the worst off the child is. This child has to act like a judge, like a psychiatrist, counselor, mediator, and a negotiator. You're forcing the kid to shoulder a huge load, depending on his age, even if he is sixteen years old or seventeen years old. It's a big load on his shoulders and it's very hard to carry. The recommendation that I give to my patients is," keep your children away from the conflicts. Hopefully, you can resolve these conflicts among yourselves. This will help the kid. But, if you have

issues, try to avoid exposing your children to them."

CUT TO:
INT. JAIL - ATTORNEY'S MEETING ROOM - DAY

          TIM

After that, she made life so miserable for my father with alimony and child support that eventually he lost everything. He wound up living in his car. One day, someone found him behind the homeless shelter with a bullet in his head. I wasn't even allowed to go to his funeral, LEENA.

CUT TO:
INT. DPI CONFERENCE - DAY

          HEIDISH

What I would mention is children have this painful kind of way too. They can be still having trouble accepting, have some anger that's residual to all of this, but I think if there's any error on that side, it's the error on the thinking that children are very resilient. If they just basically get on with their lives, there is no effect. But, all the studies show that of course there is. It may be best described as still having a significant amount of pain, maybe, and some vulnerability to very rapid change of any kind. If and when the step family situation develops over time, hearing any fighting between those parents could resurrect the feeling that this new family setting is gonna explode, and I'm gonna be caught in between. My life will be turned upside down again. So, you have a child that has trouble with conflict that may need to be reassured. But, they're resilient, somewhat, but we shouldn't over state it on that side either. So, it's sort of like we have two frames of reference. One, we think people get stuck to reality and we categorize them in any level of depression or anger, etc. And on the other hand, we over state that kids are like these bouncing balls that just keep bouncing back. I don't think either is true and both do a disservice to how we generally cope with frustrating and difficult situations.

> DR. RADFER
> In various social gatherings where one parent is absent, they question why the entire family can't put away their differences and be together? "How come they're not working harder to resolve their differences?" All these unresolved issues shatter the child's self-esteem, which is one of the most precious things a kid has. He has to deal with the fact that he has lost one of the most precious things in his life – an intact family. We know that bi-nuclei family is a viable option but to him, that is not an option. He wants them to be together. To be united, the way things are supposed to be, the way things used to be.

CUT TO:
INT. CONFERENCE ROOM 3 - DAY

> JIM
> It takes two parents to bring children into this world, and I don't see how kids can be considered happy when they're constantly being told that that's not your

> father, well you can go see him this weekend, or you can't go see him cause mommy doesn't like him, or that, that's not your real father or anything like that. When you put kids in the middle of a divorce, you're really destroying your own children, and you're destroying the moral fabric of our society for today and tomorrow.

CUT TO:
INT. DPI CONFERENCE - DAY

> KOPP
>
> Prior to being forced out of my house, I was constantly with them. I got them involved in many activities, like violin lessons, swimming, and wrestling. I participated in school activities. I went to the school after hours and helped out. I volunteered. And, I was a very active and influential parent in their lives.
>
> Unfortunately, that has now been taken away from me, and it's very hard. It's a very difficult period to go through, having your children be ripped away from you. Prior to this, there were no allegations of any wrong doing by me. It was

pretty much a normal married
family life.

BACK TO THE COURTROOM

          LEENA

These non-custodial parents were
never convicted of any
impropriety while married. Now
that they want joint custody, the
judges insist on supervised
visitation.

CUT TO:
INT. CONFERENCE ROOM 3 - DAY

          JIM

When the custody evaluation
started and the psychologist
started evaluating how we
interacted as father and sons, my
oldest one started to strike out at
me, and I asked him to sit down in
a chair, and I explained to him that
although we were in this process
together, that I was his father and
I loved him dearly. And, that's why
we were doing this, because I
wanted to be involved with him. It
was clear and evident to me, and

the psychological write up on the custody evaluation, that my kids were used as weapons, weapons in a war of divorce and custody battles which rage rampant in this nation today, and the victims are the children.

BACK TO THE COURTROOM

                LEENA

These courts often deprive the non-custodial parents equal protection of the law by failing to aggressively enforce visitation rights.

CUT TO:
INT. CONFERENCE ROOM 3 - DAY

                JIM

I wanted more with my kids other than being told I can't take them this weekend or if I did, I needed to take them ice skating or roller skating or an activity that she had planned, during my custodial visit, my court ordered custodial visit. The keyword there is court ordered. Court orders for fathers are easy to give out. There's no enforcement. Last year, I was denied Christmas, my birthday, father's day, and about two and a half months of visitation time from my court ordered agreement for my oldest son. You see, she'd come to my house with the police to pick up the kids, but the police refused to come with me to pick up my own kids during court ordered visitations. There's no right for fathers to have access to their kids. In fact the only right fathers have is to pay, and we're forced to pay. And, I don't mind paying for my children if I can see them, but I can't see them. I can't nurture them. I can't greet them off the bus from school. And, I moved five blocks away so that I can do all of those things. That's what my attorneys said would be the right thing to do if I wanted custody. They told me that those are the things that you need to do to show that you want to be a father. And, I did them all; it had no bearing what so ever on the outcome. As a matter of fact, it made things worse because it showed her I was committed to my children, a commitment that she didn't want to happen. She wanted to force me away from the lives of my children. I had a PFA filed against me, the police come to my house for assaulting her with a door that I never did. All I ever wanted to do was love my kids. I haven't seen them in six months. I haven't seen them during my court ordered visitation. I haven't talked to them on the phone through my court orders to my ex-wife to have them call me twice a week at work. None of the court orders work. Fathers don't have enforceable rights.

CUT TO:
INT. PSYCHOLOGIST'S OFFICE - DAY

          ED WILLIAMS
Let's talk about the enforcement of visitation rights. In your experience, how well are they enforced?

          JEFF
They're not. They're not. Usually, again, its cooperation between the divorced parents. The judges

issue them, but that doesn't mean that the custodial parent will comply. And, when they don't comply, your recourse is taking them back to court and doing something to get that custody law changed or change what the court has to say. Again, all these cost money, and if you don't have the economic resources to do that, then you have a problem. The other thing is that some custodial parents pack up and leave the area. Right now, I'm dealing with a case that was based in another state initially. The wife moved to Ohio, the husband moved to New Jersey, and there's nothing they can do. The wife has not seen or had custody of the children whatsoever for probably a year and a half, even though she's supposed to have shared custody for several months out of the year. There's no recourse. The only recourse you can have is at a federal level because you're crossing from state to state rather than being inside that specific state. It's fairly easy for a non-custodial parent to cross state lines, you know, and the only thing you can do in events of extreme cases is file kidnapping charges maybe at a federal level. Or hopefully, they come back to the state with the original jurisdiction and then you can have them arrested for violation of the court's custodial order. But again, they have to be caught first. So basically, there isn't a compliance mechanism in place unless you have the economic resources to enforce the custodial order. If you have the financial resources, you could hire investigators to track down the offending parent even if he or she moved to another state. A lot of times, parents come to my office depressed and upset, anxious, for not seeing their kids, and haven't seen them for a long time because the other parent is not being cooperative.

BACK TO THE COURTROOM

LEENA
The system is not any kinder to grandparents.

CUT TO:
INT. DPI CONFERENCE - DAY

>JEAN OSBORNE
>In February, my daughter came and got my granddaughter who had been living with us for five years. Three days later, she went up to the court house and secured a protective order. I understand that in Indiana on a protective order you get a hearing in 30 days. And so, we went to the courthouse and I told the judge I didn't believe there was any reason to issue a protective order, but if they wanted to issue one, I guess there was nothing I could do about it. I had been in a class at "The People's Law School" in Fort Wayne, Indiana and the teacher said when you get petitions for a protective order, they weren't worth the paper they were written on. So, I knew I didn't do anything wrong so I had nothing to fear. Well I did have something to fear because about two days after that, I took a small book to my granddaughter's school and went

to her class and gave it to her. I had been in a wreck and had many bruises on my face so I waited for a couple of weeks to deliver her birthday present so that she wouldn't be scared of my face with all the bruises on it. And so, I gave her the book at school and came back home only to be arrested the following Sunday night. While she was under our custody and living at our home. I had paid for dance lessons and her dance teacher called me and said that there was a recital. Wanting to be supportive of the child, I attended the recital and didn't have any contact with her or touch her or anything, just in the audience. The following Sunday night, I got arrested. When you get arrested in our county, they take you in the squad car and they put you in shackles and they take your picture and they take your fingerprints. I have been arrested eight times. I am now a convicted stalker. I was taken. At one point, my bond revoked for 45 days, and I was put into jail for sending a birthday card. This was devastating to me. And all through that time, I could not retain an attorney at a price that I could afford. So, I had to go to court by myself in an orange jumpsuit and shackles. And, my daughter had arranged for my granddaughter to see me in shackles and that hurt my feelings because I know that the little girl knew that I raised her and did a lot of nice things for her, and I'll bet she didn't understand why they put her grandmother in shackles. I have not seen my granddaughter to touch or hold or kiss her in years. I miss her terribly, and she's the light of my world. I can't conceive why the judicial system has not stepped in at least to help us. The state did put our granddaughter into foster care. When I called the Department of Children and Families, they gave me no answers. I asked them where my granddaughter was and they said they couldn't tell me. I couldn't understand why. You lose your wallet, you call a policeman, and if you lose your dog, you call the dog warden. You lose your grandchild and you don't know who to call. There's nobody that will give you an answer. And, you sit and wait because I haven't seen her in years. I am certain that her perspective of us has changed. They've alienated us. The system has helped my daughter alienate her from us, and I have no doubt in my mind that this is having some psychological damage to her. I know what it has done to us. We've lost all faith in the system, and we've lost all trust. That was something I never wanted to happen.

DR. HARTMAN

Too many children that are sort of cut up in this process and have fallen through the cracks to the extent that their best interests are not being served. In these sorts of proceedings, most of these children will end up in foster care placement, which the children's defense fund in Washington, D.C. has termed based on its empirical research as a national disgrace. Several commentators have also mentioned that foster care placement is essentially an unsafe haven for children. I know Prof. Michael Mushlin has published a piece in the Harvard Civil Liberties Law review that I think very poignantly captures the essence and spirit of these children's welfare proceedings and the concomitant placement of children in foster care. Prof Mushlin has found that certainly, it is ten times greater for foster care children in terms of abuse and neglect than children in the general population. Those are very much monumental findings when you think about wanting to protect children and serving their best interest and yet, in fact, we're exposing these children to higher levels of emotional and physical abuse and neglect. There are several reasons for this. For physical and sexual abuse, the incest ban that runs in biological families will not be applicable here. And, also, there may be some sort of resentment. Or, in terms of perspectives, looking at this child and the situation that this child came from within built discriminatory viewpoints and perspectives. And, I think also foster care children, to some extent, feel that they are on the outskirts of the family. That perhaps, they'll never be part of that family; there may not be very real bonding because foster care placements are thought to be very temporary.

JEAN OSBORNE

We had taken care of our granddaughter for five years out of our own pocket because we loved her. And now, she's in foster care. We would again take care of her with no compensation by state or federal grants or anything else, and we feel it's kind of a waste of the public's money to have her in foster care when we would do it for nothing. And, she would be well taken of. My husband and I don't drink. We don't use drugs. We don't gamble. We go to church and try to be good role models. I believe that she would be in good hands. But, we're having an awful time trying to prove that because there doesn't seem to be any

money in just good ole fashioned
love for a child.

CUT TO:
INT. JAIL - ATTORNEY'S MEETING ROOM - DAY

                TIM

She married again later on. She always insisted that I call him my father - refer to him as my father. I hated him!! I started having nightmares. I started drinking and experimenting with any illegal drugs you can think of.

CUT TO:
INT. DPI CONFERENCE - DAY

              DR. RADFER

He is ashamed, ashamed that he belongs to this family. They're supposed to be perfect. They're supposed to be one happy family. They were supposed to live together in harmony. How come they can't be together? "There is something wrong there. I can't let anyone find out about this." He has an element of shame. A kid with low self-esteem will not think that he deserves a good life or

being with nice friends. There will
be a lot of deterioration in his
performances in the activities he
does, and his participation will
soon decrease. This will ricochet
through most aspects of his life.

BACK TO THE COURTROOM

                LEENA
The State and the courts
abdicated their responsibilities by
tolerating parental alienation.

CUT TO:
INT. DPI CONFERENCE - DAY

              DR. RADFER
Now, he has to accept to live at
two different places. Or, if one
gets sole custody, he has to stay
with one member of the family
and spend a few hours or one or
two days with the other parent.
This really creates a lot of
problems for the child, especially
if one parent decides to program
this kid against the other side, and
if the child has to decide which
side is good or bad because of
conflicting things that the parents
are doing to undermine each

other. This really creates problems in the mind of the child. Because now, he has to revise his programing about that person, say dad. "My god, I thought he's a good dad. He took me to baseball, took me to football, he bought a lot of good things for me. How can anyone think that he's a bad or cruel person? How could he have changed so suddenly?" While the child might not realize that he was being programmed by one parent, he would still be confused by what he's being told.

DR. NEILAND
The court, in response to a petition from both sides of the case to appoint yet another mental health professional to talk with the psychiatrist, was answered by the judge appointing an attorney to function as a mental health professional and interview the psychiatrist. I had previously asked the psychiatrist only to testify in court. What she had told me over and over and over again was that my daughter wasn't the least bit afraid of me,

that she was afraid of her mother's reaction if she spent any time with me. That I had a normal loving relationship with my daughter, but the psychiatrist absolutely refused to testify. She said she simply couldn't get involved in a custody dispute, and I pointed out to her that she was required by the court order simply to respond to the question whether my daughter was afraid of me or not, that she didn't have to get involved in any kind of custody dispute. That's all the court wanted to know. Well, the attorney appointed by the court to function as a mental health professional once again met with me, met with my ex-spouse, met with the children, and met with the psychiatrist, and this led to the production of a report by the so called mental health professional, the attorney who had interviewed everyone, and, in the course of the text of the report, there were many misstatements of fact.

DR. RADFER
When the child realizes that one

parent has been feeding him lies and misrepresentation or trying to program him against the other parent, he gets angry at the programmer. "How could (say) mom be so cruel? I know that dad is a nice guy. He does a lot nice things for me. He hasn't changed; he's still the same loving father that he's always been". This anger could eventually turn into full-blown hatred or hostility.

CUT TO:
EXT. TIM IN HIS CAR - EVENING

SONG: THE FINAL STAND

Standin' in the doorway
Empty bottle in his hand
Other on the trigger
Gonna make his final stand
They call him desperado
Out on the street
Doesn't have much money
But nice boots on his feet
You may never see him smile
Only if for a little while
You may never see him cry
That final stand is the reason why

TIM (O.S.)
After, I hadn't slept for days. I remember going to the house. I parked my car on the side of the house and just sat there for more than an hour. I had a lot of pain which no amount of pain killers could ease. These pains were infused into my being. I could neither run nor hide from them. Every fucking day and every freaking night, I can't escape. I'm tired of masking the pain with whiskey and drugs. I know I wasn't going to refer to some asshole my mother picked off the street as my dad. My dad was dead!! But, on that day, things were different. I wanted to express my anger as boldly as possible. This was going to be my final stand. I had a bunch of pills and some whiskey which I wasn't going to waste. So, I sat there and chased the pills down with the whiskey. I mixed so many pills that I couldn't even remember the types or the amount. All I know is that some of them were uppers and downers. I was a complete basket case. I was so wasted.

EXT. CARMICHAEL COMPOUND – EVENING
TIM takes his gun, goes inside the house, walks to the den and sees his stepfather napping.

CUT TO:
INT. DPI CONFERENCE - DAY

>DR. NEILAND
>
>So, the net result was that I had very little time with any of my children during their childhood. I saw my son perhaps a third of the time. I hardly saw my younger daughter at all. My oldest child eventually came to live with me for several months before she went off to college but had very little actual time with her in my home during her childhood. So, the result was extremely disappointing to me. I missed out on the childhood of my children; this was time that could never be given back to me. I think the psychiatrists and the psychologists and everyone involved in this case behaved in a vile manner from the ethical point of view and subsequently, I told my story to a very able journalist

who wrote a book about my decade long saga in the family courts. The book is called "A Family Divided" by Robert Mendelson published by Prometheus Books.

FADE IN:
INT. CONFERENCE ROOM 2 - DAY

              JACOB
Growing up though, like I said, was very normal because we just thought this was how life was. I didn't realize that not having my real dad around wasn't normal until I was older. This guy, who was a friend of the family, came to be known to us as my brother's father. We were all in awe. We were teenagers then and so, I started to think about it. Hey, there's my brother's dad, there's my sister's dad, where's mine? What did I do wrong? Or, what happened between him and my mom sixteen years ago that he's not here now? I didn't know if I missed it, because I never knew how it felt to have a dad, but it just started to finally click that he

wasn't there. I honestly don't know if it would have made any difference. My mom's a pretty weak person to begin with, and I think my mom needs to be loved, and I don't think it matters who. Back then, I don't think it mattered who loved her just as long as she was with somebody. So, why all the secrecy about my dad and this that and the other, I don't know. I got different stories from different people. My grandmother told me that she liked the guy. He was a good guy, worked in the factory like everybody else and did a good job. My mom just didn't want anything to do with him. When my brother finally started having a relationship with his father, I guess I wanted to have one with mine. So, I wrote a couple letters and sent them to an address that I was told was his mother's. I never got a response. So, one day I called his mom's phone number and he happened to be at his moms. I told him who I was and I said my mom said you're my dad. He just exploded on the phone.

He's like "she's a whore, she's a liar .You know she used to sleep with everyone. Anybody could be your dad. If you call here or try to contact me again, I'll beat the hell out of you, beat the hell out of her." At that point, it was like screw you, I don't care. I don't care anymore because the way it is. I'm just destined to be without parents because my mom is with this guy and my dad doesn't want me. So, I talked to my mom about it and she just said, "See, I told you he was like that." I asked her if she was sure this guy was my real dad because he said he's not. Her answer was "I'm pretty sure." So, now I don't know if this guy is my real dad. What do you do? I don't know if my mom misled me or just flat out lied. But, whatever happened between the two of them, or whoever he is, I guess I'll never know 'cause to this day still, this is a subject we don't touch; we don't talk about it. She just tells me your step dad was more of a father than this guy would have ever been.

CUT TO:
INT. JAIL - ATTORNEY'S MEETING ROOM - DAY

                TIM
> You know the rest of the story. I stumbled into the house believing that everyone in that home was my enemy. My mother, my sisters, my bastard stepfather; all of them. They were all my enemies!

CUT TO:
INT. THE CARMICHEAL'S HOUSE - EVENING

We follow TIM inside. He finds his step dad napping on the couch. Tim fires two shots at his head, killing him instantly. He proceeds to the dining room and finds one of his sisters doing her homework and listening to some music through her head phones. TIM fires a shot and hits her on the temple. TIM goes to the living room looking for the rest of the family, but finds no one. He goes toward the hallway adjoining the steps leading to the bedrooms.

            SONG: THE FINAL STAND
There are marks on his body
That come and go
He says it's from a fall he took
Thinks that we don't know
How his stepfather treats him
Its love they lack

He tells his stepfather
One day I'll pay you back

You may never see him smile
Only if for a little while
You may never see him cry
That final stand is the reason why

An angel called this morning
Said son it's time to go
Turmoil in his heart
Whiskey soaked so it won't show
In the black of night
Tim came to stake a claim
Home built by his father
And taken by another's name

CUT TO:
TIM's younger SISTER opens her bedroom door and rushes down the steps with her cell phone in one hand, trying to call for help. TIM walks into frame with the gun pointed at her. Her deafening scream is quieted by three rapid fire shots from TIM.

CUT TO:
INT. JANE'S BEDROOM – LATE EVENING

JANE is in her bed sleeping.

TIM slowly opens the door and walks in. He sees his mother sleeping and pauses for a few seconds. He raises his gun and fires at his mother. But, to his disappointment, the only noise emanating from his weapon was the click of an empty chamber. He tries firing again, unconvinced that all his six bullets were spent. The incessant quivering of his hands betrays an admixture of nervousness and emotional turbulence as he checks his pockets for the dropped bullet. He opens the chamber and places the bullet in the ascendant well. TIM cradles his gun with both hands and presses it flat against his chest as if in a protective embrace. He gazes at his mother while lamenting the mismanagement of his munitions and pondering a solution. He wakes up his mother.

                    TIM

Momma! Momma! Wake up.
What should I do momma?

His mother wakes up.

                    JANE

What are you doing here? TIM!
What are you doing with that gun?

                    TIM

What should I do Momma? I have
only one bullet left. Who should
get it? You, or me?

Jane couldn't believe her eyes. She pulls the comforter up to her bosom as she sits up on the bed.

JANE
Put the gun down son. Let's talk about it. Put the gun down.

TIM
Momma who should get it? I got you; I got me, and only one freaking bullet.

JANE
What are you on, TIM?

TIM
A few uppers, downers, Prozac, and some whiskey. Momma, its OK, ain't it?

JANE
Where is your father?

TIM points the gun at his mother's head and fires the last bullet at her. The bullet hits her on the forehead. Blood is oozing out of the bullet wound as she falls back on the bed. Untempered by any trace of remorse, TIM leans over his dying mother and started yelling:

TIM
He's not my fucking Dad! Stepfather! Stepfather! Do you hear that Momma? Damn,

> Momma!! I'm trying to be the freaking good guy, but you just had to make me mad!!

CUT TO:
INT. JAIL - ATTORNEY'S MEETING ROOM - DAY

> TIM
> I wanted to kill myself too, but I didn't have any more bullets. There are never enough bullets.

LEENA leans over the table and hugs him.

BACK TO THE COURTROOM

> JUDGE
> Does the State have anything to say?

> PROSECUTOR
> The defendant's video brief does nothing to change the fact that MR. TIM OLSON killed his mother and other family members in cold blood. This song and dance only confirms that: one, MR. OLSON confessed, and two, that he's a remorseless monster.

> LEENA
> The prosecutor is missing the

point. Remorse is an attribute of sane minds, and its absence is symptomatic of diminished mental capacity. MR. OLSON is the creation of the State. The State failed to provide Mr. OLSON with a well-rounded nurturing environment. He's also a victim. By condemning him to death, the Court is punishing the victim while the guilty go free.

                JUDGE
Does the PROSECUTOR have anything to add?

              PROSECUTOR
No, your Honor.

DISSOLVE TO:
EXT. COURTHOUSE LAWN - DAY

DISSOLVE TO:
INT. THE COURTROOM - DAY

                JUDGE
I find the issue raised by your video brief quite compelling. This court is convinced that MR. TIM OLSON is a de facto ward of the state. He became a ward of the

> state when the courts interjected themselves into young OLSON's life, substituting its own wishes for those of his father. I also find that the State acted without regard to the wellbeing of young OLSON. MR. OLSON, as a victim, deserves treatment and apology from the State, not punishment. I therefore vacate the judgment of this court in State versus OLSON and order that the defendant be committed to Bayland Psychiatric Hospital until he's cured of his mental ails at which time, he shall be released. This court is adjourned.

The judge strikes the gavel.

BAILIFF

All rise.

The JUDGE leaves the court. LEENA is embraced by well-wishers.

CUT TO:
INT. LEENA'S OFFICE - DAY

LEENA is on the telephone.

LEENA
ROSE, guess what? We won.

ROSE
Congratulations. You're one hell of a lawyer.

LEENA
I can't wait to share this news with him.

ROSE
I'm glad that you won, but do you think that justice was done? You won freedom for the killer of a woman, his own mother for Christ's sakes. Every year, thousands of women are abused, assaulted, maimed, and murdered by men. Now, you are bashing his mother and siding with the enemy.

LEENA
I am fighting for the rights of women in second marriages. Often, the first wives take all the money, leaving their ex-husbands destitute. The women that marry these men are forced to do without enough money to cover basic needs. Some courts even

> order the second wives to give
> portions of their own income to
> the first wives. I'm fighting to
> change this. Why would you think
> otherwise? Look, but I got to go.
> Maybe we can talk about this
> later. I'll call you.

LEENA enters the jail complex. She walks through the main door across the lobby and over to the front desk. An ASSISTANT WARDEN goes to her.

SONG: THE FINAL STAND

Picture on the wall
Tim's once loving place
Before it became his hellish home
Talk about a man's case
The court did him wrong
But they had to shove
That day he flew away
Just like a morning dove

You may never see him smile
Only if for a little while
You may never see him cry
That final stand is the reason why

> ASST. WARDEN
> MS. THOMPSON, are you here
> for your client?

                    LEENA
          Yes.

CUT TO:
INT. CELLS ROW - DAY

The ASSISTANT WARDEN takes her through the corridor into a cell. In the cell, they discover TIM OLSON's body hanging from the ceiling. His bed sheet forms a noose around his neck.

                    LEENA
          Noooooooo!!!!

                    ASST. WARDEN
          Get the medics and an ambulance
          right away.

The emergency siren goes off. Three guards rush in and cut TIM loose. LEENA rushes in and buries her face on his chest sobbing.

FADE OUT

THEATRICAL CREDITS

Produced, Written, and Directed by

Pius A. Uzamere

Asst. Director .... Frances Mars

Makeup Effects .... Michelle Hanna

Camera Operator .... Bill Hinzman
1st Assistant Camera .... Heidi Hinzman

Boom Operator .... Jeff Hamilton

Special Effects .... Michelle Hanna

Partial Cast

Rhonda G. Hartman, J.D .... as herself
Maurice Heidish, MSW, LSW .... as himself
Robert Howland, M.D. .... as himself
Douglas Kopp .... as himself
Michael Nieland, M.D. .... as himself
Jean Osborne .... as herself
Fred Radfer, M.D. .... as himself

"Dennis B." .... as himself
"Jacob" .... as himself
"Jim" .... as himself
Jeff Bowen, LISW, M. Ed. (Psych)........... as himself

Music Performed by The Mighty Hellbenderz Band
Additional Music By Zero Free Music, Los Angeles
David Wurst, BMI

Academic Presentations

Post Separation Trauma and Healing After Divorce
A Presentation by Dr. Robert Howland, M.D.
Psychiatrist

The Adverse Effects of Sole Custody on Children
A Presentation by Dr. Fred Radfer M.D.
Psychiatrist

Beyond Best Interests: The Constitution and Fundamental Rights
Presentation by: Rhonda G. Hartman, J.D.
Attorney and Professor of Law

Alternative Conflict Resolution Techniques In Custody, Visitation and Other Matters
Presentation by Maurice Heidish, MSW, LSW
Social Worker

Family Courts and Child Development
An Interview with Jeff Bowen
Psychologist and Clinical Social Worker

All interviews, comments, opinions, etc. have been edited, abridged, and capsulized for time, story content, and relevancy.

Forced Absence Original Soundtrack Available on iTunes, Amazon, CD Baby and other fine retailers worldwide

Words Unspoken
Performed by The Mighty Hellbenderz Band
featuring Debbie Varney-Simon
Composed by
Randall Bass, ASCAP and Gregory Wormley,
ASCAP
Courtesy of EEC Records
Published By Des-Maraf Music Publishing Co,
ASCAP

Take It Away
Composed and Performed by The Mighty
Hellbenderz Band
Randall Bass, ASCAP and Gregory Wormley,
ASCAP
Courtesy of EEC Records and Interactives
Published By Des-Maraf Music Publishing Co,
ASCAP

I Remember
Composed and Performed by The Mighty
Hellbenderz Band
Randall Bass, ASCAP and Gregory Wormley,
ASCAP
Published By Des-Maraf Music Publishing Co,
ASCAP

The Final Stand
Composed and Performed by The Mighty
Hellbenderz Band
Randall Bass, ASCAP, and Gregory Wormley,
ASCAP

Forced Absence / 140

Courtesy of EEC Records and Interactives
Published By Des-Maraf Music Publishing Co,
ASCAP

True Story
Composed and Performed by The Mighty
Hellbenderz Band
Randall Bass, ASCAP and Gregory Wormley,
ASCAP
Courtesy of EEC Records and Interactives
Published By Des-Maraf Music Publishing Co,
ASCAP

What Am I Supposed To Do?
Composed and Performed by The Mighty
Hellbenderz Band
Randall Bass, ASCAP and Gregory Wormley,
ASCAP
Courtesy of EEC Records and Interactives
Published By Des-Maraf Music Publishing Co,
ASCAP

Separate Ways - Forced Absence Theme
Composed and Performed by The Mighty
Hellbenderz Band
Music by Randall Bass, ASCAP and Gregory
Wormley, ASCAP
Courtesy of EEC Records and Interactives
Published By Des-Maraf Music Publishing Co.

www.ingramcontent.com/pod-product-compliance
Lightning Source LLC
Chambersburg PA
CBHW071500080526
44587CB00014B/2163